LIVING

AT THE

LEADING

EDGE

OF

CHANGE

A Leader's Guide to Transition Management

WILLIAM J. MORIN
ROBERT W. LEWIS

DBM
PUBLISHING

A DIVISION OF DRAKE BEAM MORIN, INC.

Requests for permission to make copies of any part of the
work should be mailed to: Permissions, DBM Publishing,
a Division of Drake Beam Morin, Inc., 100 Park Avenue,
New York, NY 10017 or 1-800-345-5627, FAX 212-972-2120.

Cover photograph by World Perspectives/Tony Stone Images
Book design by Katrinka Blickle

Printed and bound in the United States of America
ISBN 1-880030-45-4

CONTENTS

INTRODUCTION

MANAGING CHANGE is both a business and a way of life at Drake Beam Morin, Inc.

Ten years ago we first identified an opportunity to help our clients humanize the major change initiatives so many organizations were undertaking. At the time, we identified our company in terms of what historically had been our primary line of business: career transition and outplacement counseling. As we assessed the needs of our clients, and analyzed the skills and experience housed within our own organization, we saw that we could and should operate — and define ourselves — in terms of a broader environment, one that encompassed all aspects of career and change management.

And so, systematically and strategically, we set out to fundamentally change and redefine DBM.

At first we thought the process would be straightforward. It didn't take long to realize (and, in hindsight, it should have come as no surprise) that, even for a company working with change on a daily basis, there is nothing automatic, immediate, or simple about dealing with major organizational change. In fact, as we worked to transform our company, it's safe to say that we gained personal experience with every challenge, opportunity, pressure point, and misconception described in this booklet.

We were especially lucky in one respect: because of our work in the field, we possess invaluable real-world awareness of the change process. Our change management professionals reassured us that the things we were feeling, confronting, and at times enduring were natural effects of the change process. When productivity suffered, a morale issue surfaced, or life seemed particularly chaotic, we could interpret these events not as signs that our world was falling apart but as natural consequences of change. Eventually we understood that these conditions indicated we were making progress toward our goal.

On a personal level, living with change at DBM has made me uniquely aware of the special challenges and demands change requires of leaders. To take advantage of the perceived opportunities that prompt change, some leaders feel an urge to hurry the process along. And, in fact, leaders need to be resolute and tireless champions of change for the process to succeed. We may not realize, however, that if we get too far ahead of the organization we can slow or even defeat change rather than accelerate it.

My own experience has been that — at some point in the journey from the old to the new in any organization — leaders almost inevitably wonder to themselves, "What's taking everyone so long?" What I've come to understand is that this is not cause for panic but a signal to move back into the organization, meeting people where they are in the change process, encouraging them to keep pushing ahead, assuring them that we can't and won't go back on our plans, and reassuring them about the future and the ultimate success of our efforts.

We haven't finished with change at DBM. I don't believe we ever will be. Throughout our organization and among our clients, it has grown clear that change isn't a one-time phenomenon but a permanent business partner. Today, the successful conclusion of one change initiative is more likely to be accompanied by the identification of yet other necessary changes. Our goal has shifted from surviving change to becoming change-hardy or change-resilient as an organization.

Both as individuals and as organizations, the good news is we can substantially improve our ability to deal with change. As our understanding of the change process improves, we continue to find new ways to reduce the depth and duration of the disruption that typically accompanies it, making the process far more predictable and far less eventful. We begin to understand that change is a natural part of our personal and professional lives. We begin to interpret it as an ally in our efforts to propel organizations forward to enjoy future success.

I hope that this booklet will serve you as a useful introduction to these possibilities.

William J. Morin
Chairman, Drake Beam Morin, Inc.
New York, 1995

THE

challenge

OF

CORPORATE

CHANGE

THIS IS what happened to a small MIS department in a big corporation after the company's CEO announced a reorganization.

One of the department's systems analysts quit the company to find a position with, as he put it, "a secure employer." The two analysts who remained shouldered their departed colleague's workload along with their own and helped train a new employee. Several deadlines were missed, and one project had to be subcontracted to an outside vendor.

THE HIDDEN COSTS OF UNMANAGED CHANGE

A programmer analyst threatened to leave the department and was given a pay raise to stay. Two other programmer analysts each took six sick days within a two-month period, started job searches, and became active contributors to a rumor mill that began to thrive within the department. A secretary "quit and stayed," reporting for work each day — but not doing any — while fertilizing the negative environment that was spreading through the department.

The manager of the MIS department, consumed with employment interviews, contractor management duties, morale issues, training demands, and performance-coaching responsibilities, found that she could devote only half of each week to her traditional work responsibilities.

A human resources manager quantified the costs of the disruption and discovered that, during a 60-day period, the MIS department incurred more than $65,000 of unanticipated expenses.

ANALYST REPLACEMENT (WITH AGENCY FEE)	$17,000
REPLACEMENT SALARY INCREASE	666
OUTSOURCED PROJECT	27,000
TEMPORARY CLERICAL	675
MANAGER DRAIN (50%)	5,250
EMPLOYEE PRODUCTIVITY LOSS (20%)	10,000
SICK DAYS	690
EAP USE	3,000
COUNTER OFFER/RAISE	800
	$65,081

There is nothing unusual about change costing companies money. What makes this incident interesting is that the members of the MIS department had been told, in person and in advance, that *none of them* would be affected at all by the reorganization. No one would be terminated or reassigned; all positions were secure.

Assuming the members of the group would feel relieved and might even respond to this apparent vote of confidence with a show of increased effort and improved productivity, management turned its attention to what were assumed to be the company's "problem" areas.

Change
turns out
this way
all too often.

It doesn't have to.

THE CASE FOR MANAGED CHANGE

In fact many organizations muster the resolve to manage change aggressively and effectively only *after* the pain of a particularly difficult change effort makes leaders resolve to act differently the next time they confront change.

For the St. Francis Regional Medical Center in Wichita, Kansas, a mid-1980s downsizing was, in the words of the hospital's CEO, "a horrible experience for those who went and those who stayed." More recently, as conditions in the health care industry changed dramatically in the early 1990s, hospital management realized that, to succeed in the new environment, the organization would have to redefine its corporate culture. The only way to change the culture, the CEO reasoned, "was to change everything." This time, however, she was determined to do things differently.

She wasn't dabbling with cosmetic change. Disregarding existing systems and practices, an "ideal" management structure was mapped out for the medical center. Job titles were defined, but the people who would hold them were not identified. The old structure was simply dissolved, and everyone who had been involved in managing the hospital was invited to apply for whatever new

position he or she felt best qualified to fill.

**The result,
the CEO remembers,
"was terror,
confusion, upheaval,
and little by little,
understanding,
cooperation, and
success."**

The trip from terror to
cooperation and success
is not a random voyage:

- Two years of planning preceded the actual announcement of change.

- By the time the formal change announcement was made, the entire process had been carefully planned and developed with the help of outside consultants.

- A comprehensive needs assessment was conducted.

- A time line for all changes was created.

- A script for the CEO's general announcement of change was developed.

- The CEO was coached on effective ways to deliver her message; an emphasis was placed on ensuring that the staff understood her to be fair and upfront with news.

- At the reorganization announcement meeting (held in June 1993 and attended by more than 400 upper-level staff members), each employee was given a bound, 80-page booklet containing a vision statement, a new organization chart, a time table for the reorganization, fact sheets, copies of all position descriptions, and a question-and-answer section.

- Letters about the restructuring were sent to the homes of all hospital employees.

- All management personnel attended mandatory seminars on change management conducted by outside consultants.

- A weekly newsletter kept employees informed about the change effort throughout the process.

- A huge organization chart was posted in the hospital cafeteria. As each position was filled, the individual's name and photograph was added to the chart (and published in the newsletter).

- In August, on the first official day of the new organizational structure, all employees received a flower accompanied by a note saying, "Today starts a new beginning focused on you."

- "New Beginnings" banners were strung up over doors and entryways.

- To underscore the organization's rebirth, the details of old ways of doing things were changed. Standard dates and times for regular hospital meetings, and even the names of the meetings, were revised, for example.

- At the end of September, on the day the new structure was completely in place, a company picnic was held for all employees.

- Communications continued. Another newsletter was created to keep people attuned to the organization's cultural changes.

- Bi-weekly manager feedback sessions assessed the ongoing success of the reorganization.

Today the St. Francis Regional Medical Center has 200 fewer managers than before its reorganization, and hospital operations are running stronger and smoother than ever. The management team is a close-knit unit. Decisions are made at much lower levels than in the past. Good ideas are no longer strangled by red tape. The organization is more fluid than in the past, continually adapting to continual change.

THE "STANDARD" CHANGE EXPERIENCE

EXAMPLES OF successful change management like the St. Francis Medical Center experience are not common. Time and again, careful analysis and pre-para-tion are subverted by unforeseen events with the result that organizations fail to benefit from, or even complete, ambitious change efforts. Ultimately, the best many can do is struggle to revert to the status quo, regaining what they had originally planned to leave behind.

Trouble appears when leaders assume that organizations possess an innate ability to look after themselves and adjust automatically to **change.**

THERE CAN be no doubt that change is consuming business today. Mergers and acquisitions, downsizings, rightsizings, reorganizations, realignments, redeployments, restructurings, re-engineerings, corporate reinventions, new strategies, new "cultures": the menu of change options continues to grow as companies work to find ways to respond effectively to new competition and changing economic realities.

"WE DIDN'T MAKE THE RIGHT DECISION"

 Mergers are notorious for being very difficult to accomplish successfully... Any time you go through a merger there is change, and nobody likes change.

The results of so much change do not always meet **expectations.**

- Seventy-five percent of a sample of 500 companies reported a collapse of morale when a change effort was initiated.

- Two-thirds reported no increase in efficiency.

- Forty percent of the employees who remained at the "changed" companies admitted they "think regularly about quitting." (This data was collected in 1992, when job opportunities were slim to non-existent in many sectors of the economy.)

- In another survey, only 46% of companies interviewed indicated the downsizing efforts they had undertaken ultimately met expense-reduction goals.

- Less than one-third achieved profit goals.

- Only 21% reported increases in shareholder return on investment.

- Management credibility dropped by an average of 35%.

Reduced productivity, rising costs, high turnover rates, poor morale, increased absenteeism, even vandalism, sabotage, or workplace violence — these and other corporate ills have become the unintended by-products of unmanaged or inadequately managed change.

Employees feel cheated. A thirty-year veteran of one company (who, nearing retirement, felt able to speak frankly), aired a common complaint: "Senior management no longer has the interest of the employee at heart."

Managers worry about this breakdown in trust, realizing that business ultimately cannot succeed in its absence. Senior management is alarmed: "People didn't react to change the way we expected." A manager's worst fear seems to be confirmed: "We didn't make the right decision."

THE

experience

OF

ORGANIZATIONAL

CHANGE

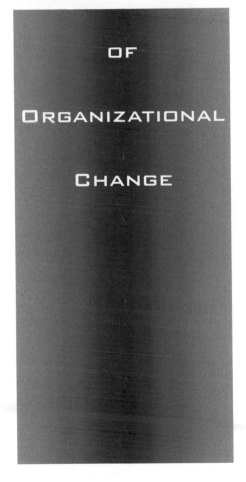

THE EARLY history of the U.S. Peace Corps demonstrates just how difficult change can be. Peace Corps leaders initially anticipated that volunteers would move into assignments enthusiastically and begin to work productively almost immediately. These were volunteers, after all, who were pursuing a "heart" issue with genuine enthusiasm and who enjoyed the general admiration of their fellow Americans.

But the leaders discovered that new Corps members typically encountered physical problems and morale issues that exceeded anyone's expectations as they struggled to integrate and adapt themselves to both the new Peace Corps culture and the cultures of the countries to which they were assigned.

**The lesson of
the Peace Corps experience is
that any substantial change —
no matter how positive, desirable,
or highly anticipated it may be —
normally produces a decline in
morale, productivity, and
commitment.**

When change isn't managed effectively, the decline tends to be immediate, steep, and substantial, as problems cut far deeper into the organization's fabric and last far longer than leaders anticipate. In the worst cases, the deterioration is irreversible, and the organization never recovers fully.

WAVES OF CHANGE

WHAT IS business to do? Unleashing major change isn't an idle corporate maneuver; competitiveness requires companies to alter their ways. It is when top management fails to institute necessary change that we read dire forecasts in the business press and watch share values decline in world financial markets.

The future looked a great deal brighter only a few years ago. Yes, employers and workers would have to adapt to new economic and competitive realities, and, yes, the process wouldn't be easy or painless. But there was an underlying feeling that, however extensive it might be, all this change would be a one-time event. Business would get "lean and mean," life would once again return to normal, and it would be back to "business as usual." A CEO might announce, "This won't be easy, but once the restructuring is complete, we'll be able to move forward into the twenty-first century with confidence...."

Most CEOs have learned to be much more temperate with their promises today, as many encounter either of two outcomes: the change effort doesn't succeed, so that the company has to retreat, regroup, and restart the process, or the successful completion of one change program demonstrates the need for additional change efforts. When change stalls or cannot be implemented quickly enough, the need for additional change often becomes apparent even before the initial change effort can be revived or completed. Successive waves of change overlap one another and overwhelm organizations.

Managers may blame the change strategies if things don't work. This can inspire a "flavor-of-the-month" mentality: "We didn't need a restructuring. What we really needed was a re-engineering." The process begins again.

Employees tend to blame the managers (although usually not to their faces). They grow skeptical and then cynical. They elect to "wait out change," lowering their heads, adopting a bunker mentality, and never buying into the change effort, because they assume that the program will not have lasting impact and will eventually be superseded by yet another round of as-yet undefined change.

If this is true — if change is a constant, continuing force to be reckoned with, and if people are responding by trying to wait things out — then the negative statistics and unfortunate experiences mentioned above aren't simply one-time problems. They turn into far more serious, long-term drags on performance, productivity, and profitability.

OPPORTUNITY COSTS COME KNOCKING

FINALLY, the opportunity cost of failing to change also merits attention. Where it was once assumed that only "sick" companies conducted change efforts, we've begun to see healthy organizations institute major reorganizations in attempts to stay in front of the curve and take advantage of change.

These companies understand that, while unmanaged or poorly managed change can produce organizational paralysis and substantial financial loss, well-managed change initiatives can create an environment of enormous business prosperity and personal opportunity.

But whether they are forced to accept change or desire to embrace it, few organizations enjoy smooth voyages.

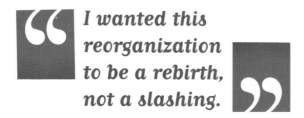

I wanted this reorganization to be a rebirth, not a slashing.

CONSIDER A hypothetical change program. Call it a restructuring. A team of top corporate managers, up to and probably including the CEO, devotes weeks or months to plan and prepare for the effort. They analyze existing conditions to determine what to do differently in the future. They consider a range of potential plans and ultimately narrow the field to the strategy they believe will produce the desired effects.

Task forces and project teams are identified and staffed to take care of details and implement the program. The change makers establish a schedule and work tirelessly to push the plan forward.

When all the pieces are finally in place, the change is introduced throughout the organization. The CEO may jet off to corporate outposts or use a satellite hook-up to announce the new structure to employees in distant locations. Local managers respond to employee concerns in carefully orchestrated question-and-answer sessions. Manuals are written and distributed. Videotapes are produced and screened.

Then the managers who have worked so hard to introduce the change breathe a collective sigh of relief and turn back to the business itself. They are reassured as a

WHEN THE TROOPS DON'T FOLLOW

few employees overtake them, rushing ahead to exploit new opportunities.

"Thank God that's over," they tell each other. "Now we can get on with our *real* work."

After a while, however, the leaders look up and around, and are confounded by what they see: *the troops aren't following*. Some people are having trouble keeping up. Others wander aimlessly. Some are motionless. A few have turned around and are marching resolutely back into the distance, 180 degrees away from change.

"What do we have to do with these people?"
the managers complain to one another.
"We told them what was happening.
Why don't they get on board?"

misconceptions

ABOUT

CHANGE

Perhaps companies and individuals find it so difficult to deal with change because so few understand accurately how change "works." Consider some common misconceptions:

1. *Change is fast.*

Change is indeed "fast" for people who embrace change. But, as we'll see, people who genuinely welcome change tend to represent a distinct minority in most organizations. Most employees are far more likely to need time to digest and accept change. Some people need a great deal of time, many need active assistance, and a few are simply never able to adapt.

2. *Time heals all wounds: stability eventually returns naturally to an organization.*

In fact, if change destabilizes an organization, the deterioration tends to continue and accelerate in the absence of forceful and effective intervention. Many organizations, having waited in vain for conditions to improve on their own, introduce their first formal change management initiatives only when senior managers realize belatedly that conditions have progressed from painful to intolerable.

3. Survivors are thankful for their jobs.

"Thankful for what?" employees wonder. Some feel "survivor's guilt" as they watch old friends and colleagues leave the organization unwillingly. Others observe, "Now they want me to do my own job plus the work of someone who's gone, but nobody's given me the resources to do that — or told me how and where to start." Major change is always accompanied by some level of organizational disorder, and few people react by thinking, "Thank you for the chaos."

4. People who do not get on board quickly are "wrong."

Different people require different amounts of time (and different types and degrees of assistance) to come to terms with change. As we'll see, a change initiative can be considered successful only when people representing a "critical mass" within the organization accept and align themselves with the new situation. Very few people complete that process quickly or intuitively, and if the message, "You're wrong," goes out to the majority of employees who need time and help to adapt and adjust, successful resolution may prove impossible.

5. People who seem okay are okay.

People who see their leaders committed to change, but who, themselves, are uncertain about — or even actively opposed to — the transformation, are more likely to hunker down than speak up. Some may even act like guerrillas, lurking in the corporate shadows and ambushing change as opportunities present themselves.

The CEO of one of the country's largest corporations, determined to redefine the way his company approached and conducted business, was astonished to find that several of his own lieutenants — the senior managers who were officially charged with pushing change throughout the organization — would agree with him in private and then go off quietly to subvert the change initiative.

6. Strong performers flourish; weak people leave the organization.

The uncertainty that accompanies significant change tends to prompt weak performers to lie low in attempts to hang on to what they have. Stronger individuals (whose strength after all, is usually the product of superior abilities and experience) are far more likely to interpret the situation as a signal to at least consider new opportunities elsewhere.

Recruiters understand this situation. In their search for talented job candidates, they tend to target organizations that have undergone significant change for as long as a year following actual change events.

7. When management talks, everyone listens.

Somewhere in the audience (often near the back of the room), someone is telling his or her peers, "Here we go again. They've given it a new name, but we all know this is going to turn out just like the last one." When people are scared and uncertain, they can become skeptical and unreasonable. Neither quality contributes to good listening.

8. Employees accept management communication at face value.

Employees are far more likely to perceive a major distinction between what management says and what management means. Particularly in organizations where the results of past change efforts have not lived up to their expectations, employees tend to be wary and skeptical of "official" communication.

9. By communicating the "right" way, management only needs to communicate once.

Like effective advertising campaigns, successful change efforts tend to be distinguished by simple, consistent messages that are communicated repeatedly. When the communicators beg, "Please don't ask me to get up and say that again," they should be congratulated for their resolve and reminded that their message is probably just beginning to be heard.

When the Ford Motor Company concluded that it would have to fundamentally transform its corporate culture to remain competitive, senior management reached an interesting and revealing decision: the company would treat the introduction of the new culture just as it had traditionally approached the announcement of a new automobile. Ford resolved to invest the same significant level of funds and resources to communicate and market the new culture internally as would be allocated to the public introduction of a Taurus or Windstar.

10. Management can mandate a "new" organization.

Management can mandate a new organization chart or dictate a new corporate structure, but that's not the same as creating a new organization. Formal structures represent only one dimension of an organization. The informal structures that develop and become entrenched over time, plus the individual relationships employees create with their colleagues and with the organization at large, also define the organization. Significant organizational change is probably impossible unless careful and extensive attention is paid to these less formal entities and relationships.

11. Redefining formal relationships in an organization changes how business is done.

Informal relationships often have much greater relevance to the conduct of business than formal structures. The success of people with reputations for "getting things done" is often attributed to their ability to "work the system," for example, which suggests that they possess skills that extend far beyond an understanding of the organization's formal structures.

12. During change, the behavior of senior management is invisible to the rest of the organization.

In fact, employees tend to scrutinize senior management behavior in times of change, looking for signs about the future or simply trying to figure out if management is really willing to "walk the talk."

When DBM learned one of its clients had timed the announcement of a restructuring to the start of a major golf tournament senior management would be attending, for example, we suggested that management consider the mixed message this would send to the organization.

 The people who had been through change workshops were mentally in a different place. They weren't angry, they had plans, they told me what they needed and what they were going to do next.

13. People interpret the pressures and reasons for change rationally.

Some people interpret change rationally, but others react emotionally to the news, considering major change in terms of personal needs, fears, and perceptions. Organizations obviously need to reach decisions for change rationally, but this shouldn't prompt management to conclude that these decisions will be perceived or interpreted rationally. Time and again, senior managers are astounded by the inventiveness and total inaccuracy of the rumors their rational choices inspire.

14. Change occurs around a definitive event.

Change can be introduced and symbolized by a definitive event, but that's just the beginning. Successful change occurs only when enough people in the organization complete a transition, making the move from the current situation to the new, desired state.

CHANGE

AND

transition

IN FACT there are actually two main components
to the broad process of change: change itself, which we
can think of as an event, and transition, which we view
as a process. Transition encompasses a period of adjust-
ment in which people come to terms with external
change. Change events can be timed and scheduled —
the announcement of a reorganization, the date on which
a corporation shuts a plant or spins off a subsidiary, the
formal merger of two companies. The transition process
is not so precise. Change can be approached as a
strategic endeavor; transition cannot. The distinctions
are significant.

Consider the difference between change and transition
by thinking about weddings and marriages. Assume that
the seemingly infinite list of details, deadlines, and decisions leading up to and including the wedding ceremony
— invitations, wedding dresses, flowers, guest lists, cater-
ers, cakes, etcetera — fall into the category of change,
with the ceremony itself representing the formal change
event. It is at this point (as so many of us learn only from
experience), that the real work begins: the transition to
married life. If the transition isn't completed successfully,
another change event typically occurs… and another
transition begins.

The key point here is this: unless a transition can be
completed successfully, change cannot work.

CRITICAL MASS

CHANGE INTRODUCES transition, the process by which — if change is to succeed — a critical mass of individuals in the organization leaves the old situation behind to embrace, or at least honestly accept, the new. For the organization, achieving critical mass is the goal of the transition process.

Critical mass typically varies from one organization to another; it isn't a numerical objective. Perhaps the only way to identify it with real certainty is in retrospect, after it has been achieved. There is a palpable sense throughout the organization that momentum has shifted or been regained and that enough people have accepted the new situation, with the collective weight of the organization inexorably bound to the company's new direction.

At this point, even though the last individual hasn't completed his or her own personal transition (and, in fact, some never will), the transition process can be called complete and the change can be rated a success.

THE INEVITABILITY OF TRANSITION

MEASURING PROGRESS toward critical mass in transitions is an imprecise exercise, because gains are linked to behavioral responses, not to the finite, analytical data with which most managers are far more comfortable. This may be why even the most astute managers, lacking a "feel" for signs of critical mass (or its absence), can have real trouble managing transitions.

Managers are often more successful and comfortable setting strategy, making decisions, and dealing with situations on the basis of quantifiable facts and measurable events. In this situation, they may focus on change and neglect transition and, therefore, the achievement of critical mass that signifies its success.

The fact is that leaders cannot neglect transitions, because change events inevitably trigger transition experiences, whether or not an organization anticipates, wants, plans for, or reacts to them.

What may be more useful to realize is that the pace, and in fact the success, of transitions — achieving critical mass — can be affected by management decisions and activities.

EVEN IF the course or pace of transition cannot be plotted precisely, successful transitions are far from being

random, uncontrolled events. Managed effectively and aggressively, the pace of transition can be accelerated and streamlined through a variety of carefully designed interventions.

This should be management's objective: to ease and accelerate transitions so that the critical mass of employees completes the shift from the old to the new with minimum disruption in a relatively short period of time.

As we've already indicated, when transitions slow or stall, completing them successfully becomes a difficult task. If transitions are slowed significantly, the need for

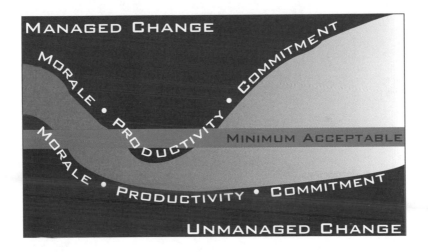

MANAGED CHANGE

MORALE • PRODUCTIVITY • COMMITMENT

MINIMUM ACCEPTABLE

MORALE • PRODUCTIVITY • COMMITMENT

UNMANAGED CHANGE

additional change may surface before the original transition can be completed. If all momentum is lost, critical mass may never be achieved, and a demotivated organization may find itself in worse shape than when it started.

An active and aggressive response by management is obviously called for. To understand how senior managers can engage the issue, we first need to understand how transitions proceed.

If we think back to the Peace Corps example, we recall that any significant change — even if it is eagerly anticipated by all involved — normally produces a decline in morale, productivity, and commitment. As the comparison of managed and unmanaged change curves illustrates, the challenge for management is to minimize the depth and duration of the decline by channeling organizational energy into defining and ultimately embracing the change. To accomplish this, managers need to expect (and indeed respect) the fact of declining productivity among employees.

TRANSITION:

THE

individual

PERSPECTIVE

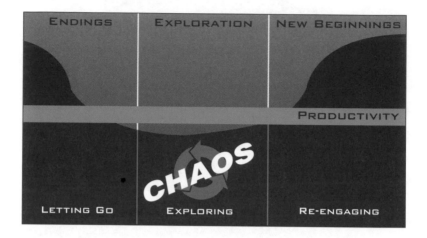

DIVIDING THE transition journey into three phases and then considering typical individual reactions and organizational responses to each stage of the process may help explain declining productivity. We call the three phases Endings, Exploration, and New Beginnings.

In the Endings phase, individuals must cope with closure — letting go of familiar things — a task that inevitably means dealing with strong emotions. People have to let go of the past, accepting the loss of old and comfortable ways.

Next comes Exploration, when individuals begin to reorient themselves to the new reality. Here is where the decline in productivity is typically greatest, as people are alternately torn between the future and the past, embracing change tentatively then recoiling back toward a familiar past. If employees do not receive adequate information and support during this period in particular, the exploration phase is likely to be characterized by chaos.

If all goes well, people eventually work their way through Exploration to enter the third phase of the transition, where they experience a sense of New Beginnings. By reaching this point, they demonstrate that they're ready to move forward in and with the new organization. They feel reasonably secure with the organization's new direction, and they can once again become significant contributors.

RIDING THE TRANSITIONAL TRAPEZE

THE IMAGE of a trapeze artist offers a good analogy for the three phases of transition.

Imagine a dream in which you find yourself standing on a platform high above the audience in a crowded circus tent. A trapeze bar swings forward and back in front of you. You've never been on a trapeze before, but the crowd urges you on.

You realize that, if you grasp the trapeze and swing out into space, the next thing you'll have to do is let go of the bar to shift to a second trapeze. The prospect raises two timely questions.

1 "Will the other bar be there when I need it? I realize that the answer to this question is out of my control, in someone else's hands, someone (gulp) I don't even know. I'll be at that person's mercy if I let go, and I'm not sure he or she has my safety at heart."

2 "Is there a net beneath me, is it in the right place, and will it support my weight?"

You take a deep breath, throw caution to the wind, grab the bar of the first trapeze, and let go, leaving the platform in search of the second trapeze. (You've completed the Endings phase of transition.)

The act of leaving the platform leaves you with an overwhelming, frantic focus on a single goal: connecting. All your senses are supernaturally alert. You look in sixteen different directions and consider as many alternatives in your search for that secure connection. You even think about heading back toward your starting point, but realize that the trapeze will no longer take you back that far. (This is precisely what people feel during Exploration.)

Finally you catch the new bar and swing safely to the far platform. You have a tremendous sense of relief, accomplishment, and excitement. (You're in New Beginnings.)

Perhaps you'll not desire to repeat the experience anytime soon, but at least you'll know you can do it. You've experienced change resilience, a quality that, from both a personal perspective and from an organizational standpoint, helps to encourage and ensure future success with change.

-------------------------------------▶ **Change resilience.**
1. A quality that helps to encourage and ensure future success with change.
2. Congratulations!
You're in New Beginnings.

THREE PHASES OF INDIVIDUAL TRANSITION

THIS GRAPHICAL catalog of typical emotional responses to the different transitional phases may explain both the hesitancy with which most people approach transitions (or trapezes) and the declining productivity that the situation inspires.

As individual employees begin the transition process, they tend to encounter an array of troublesome feelings: denial, anger, and so forth. If they are able to resolve them, they begin to let go of the past and move on to the Exploration phase, where conditions aren't much more inviting: confusion, conflict, and considerable stress emerge as people test the waters of change.

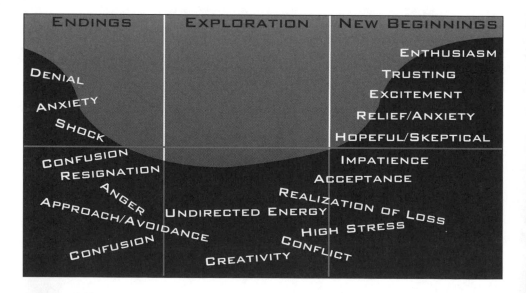

ENDINGS	EXPLORATION	NEW BEGINNINGS
		ENTHUSIASM
DENIAL		TRUSTING
ANXIETY		EXCITEMENT
SHOCK		RELIEF/ANXIETY
		HOPEFUL/SKEPTICAL
CONFUSION		IMPATIENCE
RESIGNATION		ACCEPTANCE
ANGER		REALIZATION OF LOSS
APPROACH/AVOIDANCE	UNDIRECTED ENERGY	HIGH STRESS
CONFUSION		CONFLICT
	CREATIVITY	

The real turnaround in productivity begins relatively late in the transition process, at the point of "Realization of Loss" and "Acceptance," which also signals the shift from Exploration to New Beginnings. At this point emotions tend to turn more positive, as people, realizing that there can be no turning back, reach decisions to actively participate in — or even contribute to — the change.

**At this point,
they begin to feel excitement and
enthusiasm about the future.**

TRANSITION: THE ORGANIZATIONAL PERSPECTIVE

AS INDIVIDUAL employees work their way through transitions, the view from the organization's perspective — in theory, at least — tracks their progress. Business as usual deteriorates into disorganization — even chaos — which is subsequently succeeded by revitalized performance, as declining productivity is finally reversed.

Remember, however, that both from the individual and organizational perspectives, we are speaking in terms of an ideal transition scenario. In fact there is nothing inexorable or automatic about the process. The morale/pro-

	ENDINGS	EXPLORATION	NEW BEGINNINGS
Phases of the organizational transitional process	BUSINESS AS USUAL		REVITALIZED PERFORMANCE
		DISORGANIZATION	
Phases of the individual process	LETTING GO		RE-ENGAGING
		EXPLORING	

ductivity curve doesn't turn up on its own. (Remember change misconception #2: Time does not heal all wounds; stability does not return naturally to an organization.) There is nothing preordained about individual — and, as a result, organizational — ability to move from Endings to Exploration to New Beginnings.

Management has to lead the effort.

CHAOS AND CREATIVITY;
DANGER AND OPPORTUNITY

Two phenomena surface during the Exploration phase
that create a valuable opportunity to
demonstrate leadership and push the transition along:
high levels of creativity and undirected
energy emerge at a time of considerable chaos.

The pair may actually represent two sides of the same
coin: the approach/avoidance character of this phase
not only generates disorder but, in doing so, also
inspires individuals to consider their situation in new
and previously unimagined ways, unleashing creative
ideas and impulses in the process.

We find analogies for this situation in the
natural world. Think of a forest fire, for example,
that devastates a huge, mature, and majestic expanse,
but, at the same time, opens and prepares the land
for explosive new growth, regeneration,
and rejuvenation.

WHAT

leaders

CAN

DO

FROM THE leader's perspective, the important thing to remember is that Exploration not only offers the opportunity for significant gains but also raises the specter of substantial losses. As the level of creative energy increases, management can work to direct this energy into the business and, in doing so, help people move toward the final phase of New Beginnings relatively quickly and easily. If this doesn't happen, that is, if creativity is shut down, the organization can easily become mired in destructive, rather than creative, chaos.

**The challenge for
senior managers, then,
is to enlist people to use
their heightened creativity to**
move
the change process forward.

Throughout transition, senior managers can consider and attend to a range of issues to move the process along. Listed below are the key priorities — broken down within each transitional phase — leaders should implement.

During the Endings phase, leaders need to help employees let go of the past by demonstrating awareness of their feelings and by reassuring them that the proposed changes will not devalue past contributions.

Empathy

Senior managers need to acknowledge the feelings of others in organizations confronted with change. This does not mean supporting people who simply want the entire issue of change to disappear. It does mean developing the ability to say, and mean, "I understand how you feel. I realize that change isn't easy."

Validation

When change is introduced, people tend to interpret the message as a rejection of past practice. "They're telling us we've been doing things wrong all along," employees think. "If they weren't, they wouldn't be telling us we need to change."

People need validation from the top of the organization in this situation. They need to understand that what they've done in the past was good, not bad. It was right for the time, but times have changed, and now new approaches are called for.

Employees also need to be told that they can make mistakes and still survive in the organization's new and hectic environment. A key learning point for all concerned is realizing that senior management will make decisions with no guarantee of the outcome. There will be failures, and the entire organization needs to decide that that's okay.

EXPLORATION

Knowledge is a particularly valuable commodity during the Exploration phase. The more information that can be communicated effectively, the greater peoples' ability to develop new and good ideas in an environment of positive chaos. Transitions are not times for official hemming and hawing. Information needs to be clear and unequivocal. At least one precept should be carved in stone: Going back is not an option.

Information

In the absence of accurate information about the need for, process of, and progress toward change, people inevitably think the worst. If they are told the truth, even if the news is bad, it will not be nearly as bad as what they would imagine in an information vacuum.

Communication

Leaders need to be good communicators, which, because effective communication is as much an act of active listening as talking, is not the same as being good information sources. Distributing a memo is not communicating; listening actively for employee reactions is.

Structure

The Exploration phase of transition is also the time when structure needs to be introduced, or re-introduced, to the organization. As employees let go of the past, gaining a clear sense of how the future will look helps them re-engage with the future.

NEW BEGINNINGS

Key priorities associated with New Beginnings are actually vital throughout all phases of transition but become particularly important if the process is to be completed successfully.

Participation

Leaders need to set a tone by vigorously participating in the transition, and then, just as importantly, they need to encourage the participation of others and empower them to do the job effectively.

With the help of video conferences, videotapes, and support materials, DBM trained 8,000 managers to talk to an employee population of 100,000 people. A comment on one manager's voluntary feedback form summed up general impressions of the effort: "For the first time in twenty years, this organization has really trusted me to be a manager. Thank you."

Alignment

Leaders need to take the organization's pulse continuously during transitions, shifting resources, rearranging initiatives, and fine-tuning activities so that the elusive critical mass of employees complete their individual transitions as quickly, and with as little pain, as possible.

All these priorities demand senior executive time and attention. If a senior manager's to-do list looks the same during a transition as it did before the change, then he or she isn't doing the right thing. While leaders need to fight the urge to do everything themselves, they also need to make their presence a key ingredient — almost an icon or emblem — for the comprehensive transition process.

On a tactical level, a leader's priorities during transition might look something like this:

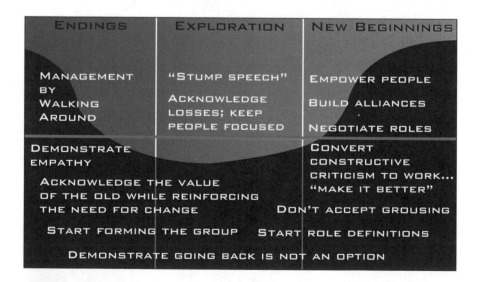

ENDINGS	EXPLORATION	NEW BEGINNINGS
MANAGEMENT BY WALKING AROUND	"STUMP SPEECH" ACKNOWLEDGE LOSSES; KEEP PEOPLE FOCUSED	EMPOWER PEOPLE BUILD ALLIANCES NEGOTIATE ROLES

DEMONSTRATE EMPATHY

CONVERT CONSTRUCTIVE CRITICISM TO WORK... "MAKE IT BETTER"

ACKNOWLEDGE THE VALUE OF THE OLD WHILE REINFORCING THE NEED FOR CHANGE

DON'T ACCEPT GROUSING

START FORMING THE GROUP   START ROLE DEFINITIONS

DEMONSTRATE GOING BACK IS NOT AN OPTION

WHAT

LEADERS

CAN

be aware

OF IN

THEIR

ORGANIZATIONS

PERCEPTION = REALITY

WHEN SITUATIONS are not well-defined or seem chaotic, which is typically the case for employees when organizations introduce significant change, people tend to respond by turning inward and becoming preoccupied with their own needs.

Perception equals reality in these situations. It's not what's done or intended that matters, it's what people believe was done or intended. Preoccupied with their own needs, they focus their perceptions at a very personal, even selfish, level. If employees decide they aren't being told the truth, they are likely to feel threatened. Unless and until they resolve their "Me" issues, they are unlikely to focus their energies on anything but work.

So, if senior management wants employees to commit to change in this environment, careful attention to "Me" concerns also becomes a priority.

LEADERS MAY have their own "Me" issues to consider. Some may have trouble distinguishing between feelings and fact, for instance. If we feel fear, we believe

there is something to fear, and we react accordingly. If we feel anger, we decide that we need to attack something, and we do.

A typical managerial trait is the conviction that leaders should set higher expectations for themselves than for the people who work for them. If things aren't going "right," their response becomes, "Okay, then, we'll do it my way." The unstated message is that "their" way is the best, or even, the only way.

During transitions, particularly during the chaos of Exploration, managers are likely to feel that the situation is out of control when in fact the sense of chaos really means that transition is proceeding according to schedule. If there is no sense of chaos, that may indicate an organization has yet to progress beyond the Endings phase of the transition.

THE CONTROL MONSTER

ONCE MANAGERS identify disorganization, how do they respond to this inevitable part of transition? They decide, "I feel out of control, so the situation must be out of control. If I don't regain control, we'll have a real disaster. Let's do it my (the best and only) way."

What happens to the creativity that is concurrently percolating up throughout the organization? Management shuts it down.

We recall the experience of one company when it encountered chaos while dealing with significant change. Management had started down a promising track, talking about empowerment and challenging their employees to "take ownership" of the business. Employee teams were assembled and granted authority to deal with specific needs and opportunities. The environment began to kindle creativity and enthusiasm. Teams even began to meet before work to address challenges.

After a few weeks, the company's president reviewed some financial data and determined that corporate expenses seemed out of line. His response was classic: "If I don't get these expenses back under control, we'll be in deep trouble." One item in particular caught his eye. Those teams holding early morning meetings were ordering breakfast from a fast-food outlet.

The president sent out a directive to thousands of employees in his company that said, in effect, "From now on, when you have meetings, if you're going to order doughnuts, the request must go through my office." The memo turned the organization upside down.

The president wasn't really worried about doughnuts, of course. He was haunted by feelings of chaos and loss of control. That's understandable, particularly for individuals who have climbed to the top of the organizational ladder by being in control and making everyone and everything respond to and respect the "one right way."

This situation wasn't part of the change plan, however, but a personal reaction to feelings. And, unfortunately, it marked the start of an unintended process of changing the change that the organization wanted to make in the first place.

The incident reveals that senior managers are actually humans: they live out their own transitions just like everyone else. As an individual, the president found himself in Exploration, where, not unnaturally, he encountered common reactions of approach and avoidance. On one day the change effort seemed great, his company was solving problems left and right, things were getting done, and progress was being made. On the next day, the expense picture had gone haywire, the organization was on the brink of disaster, and all hell broke loose.

TRANSITION

misalignment:

WHEN THE

TROOPS

DON'T

FOLLOW

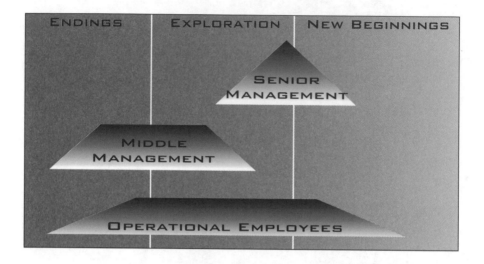

NOT REALIZING where people are in transitions or what their needs might be is another way in which leaders don't just fail to enhance the process but actually delay or sabotage it. We call the situation "transition misalignment."

By the time change is formally announced (when most members of the organization will be entering the Endings phase of transition), senior managers tend to be focused on New Beginnings. They've digested the situation and, as we suggested earlier, want to get on with business. As a result, they may show little awareness of, or demonstrate scant empathy for, the transition status and needs of others in the organization.

Middle managers often find themselves stuck in the initial, Endings phase of the transition process. Change has not been kind to middle management in recent years, so its members may intuitively and understandably sense that they have a great deal at risk. That can prompt them to try to cling to the past.

The situation creates a recipe for organizational gridlock. Senior managers can't understand why so many lag so far behind. Middle managers try to dig in, stop time, and conserve what they have. The rest of the organization wonders what on earth the higher-ups are doing.

INNOVATORS, ADAPTERS, AND THE STATUS QUO

As illustrated by senior managers who admit the need to change and then go off to fight the process tooth and nail, misalignment is likely to occur within organizational layers as well.

People are individuals before they are managers or employees. Faced with change, they tend to self-select into one of three groups. Roughly 20 percent tend to be Innovators, those individuals who embrace change naturally and who observe, "It's about time."

Another 20 percent or so form the Status Quo. At best these people find it terribly difficult to adapt to change, and some are simply unable to complete transitions.

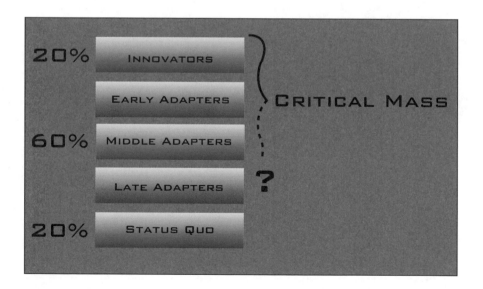

The remaining 60 percent, the middle of the organization, are Adapters. They can be further divided into Early, Middle, and Late Adapters, labels that refer to the relative ease with which they deal with change. Transitions are more or less benign events for Early Adapters while Late Adapters have considerable trouble completing them. They differ from members of the Status Quo, however, in that while it may be difficult for them they do have the capacity to complete transitions.

ADAPTERS: THE KEY TO CRITICAL MASS

WHILE RATIOS shift from one organization to another, the deviation is never enough to invalidate an obvious conclusion: an organization's ability to achieve critical mass in a transition rests with its Adapters. The challenge for senior management is to move the Adapters in the direction of the Innovators to accelerate the process of gaining critical mass. If, instead, the Adapters take the direction of the Status Quo, critical mass may never result, and the transition may never be completed.

> **Leaders who**
> **want change to succeed**
> **need to find ways to**
> ------------------► **enable the Innovators,**
> ------------------► **enlist the Adapters,**
> ------------------► **and help the Status Quo**
> **find a more appropriate fit — either within**
> **the organization or someplace else.**

To accomplish this, senior management must realize that individuals will respond to events from different vantage points, with different perceptions, and at different times.

IF LEADERS want the organization as a whole to complete the transition successfully, senior managers need to focus on aligning the

organization; they should serve as champions of alignment by understanding that the transition experience doesn't take place on a one-way street. As individuals approach and then avoid change, one step forward is often followed by two steps back. Managers who treat this as a failure, or as an example of "not getting on board," are likely to antagonize individuals and exacerbate misalignment.

To be effective, management activity has to correspond to the transition phase in which employees find themselves. Acknowledging the value of old ways can be very useful for people who are moving through the Endings stage of transition, for example, because it can help them deal with the feelings of denial, anger, and confusion that are common then. But offering the same validation to someone who is in the New Beginnings phase is probably useless and may actually be counterproductive. This individual doesn't need to hear about the past, but should be encouraged to fertilize a growing sense of enthusiasm for the future.

If, on the other hand, management focuses on negotiating new work roles and building alliances — New Beginnings priorities — for people who are still struggling to leave the Endings phase, either the message won't make sense or will be perceived negatively: "I'm struggling with what feels like a death in the family, and they're all crowing about a rosy future. They don't have a clue about what's really going on."

No wonder senior managers have trouble dealing with change and transition! How on earth can they hope to attend to all these needs?

The obvious answer is that they can't. But for many top managers the lesson to be learned is anything but obvious and is likely to be threatening: they need to be willing to relinquish control.

Leaders don't align organizations in transition by going out and aligning them. Organizations have to align themselves. The leader's role should be to support and provide resources for that process.

In times of transition, individuals feel a consuming need to interact with people in power, the folks who know what's really going on. If they think that only the CEO fits this job description, then they believe that they need to see the CEO more often than ever. Unless he or she runs an organization of, say, ten people or less, no CEO can fill this role. What leaders can do, however, is invest others with accurate information, direct them to communicate with the organization, and then seek their feedback about relevant issues and concerns.

LETTING GO

creating

A

New

employer/employee

Contract

THE ACCELERATING incidence and pace of change has also underlined a broader issue for organizations: the realization that the traditional employer/employee relationship — where people expected an assumed right to permanent employment, "paying" for the privilege by letting employers control their careers — is no longer in effect.

Business understands that it can't afford to assure the destiny of employees. And while most employees probably acknowledge the reasons for this on an intellectual level, many feel betrayed on a visceral, emotional level. ("Senior management no longer has the interest of the employee at heart.")

Loss of trust has serious implications for companies in change. If employees don't trust management, then management can't expect optimum (or perhaps even acceptable) performance. When companies are in the midst of major change, trust becomes a critical issue.

Leaders need to encourage the people they do trust by offering support and resources, for example, when these individuals encounter trouble. Likewise, leaders need to level with people they *don't* trust. If managers don't deliver these messages properly, they may unintentionally inspire paranoia in those who are worthy of trust while shepherding those who are not.

A few companies have begun to develop a new kind of

employer/employee contract, one which is based on a new form of "nondependent" trust which empowers workers by giving them control of their careers. It expands the concept of change hardiness into career resiliency.

This is an agreement between the organization and the employee based on current economic and competitive reality. The employee gives up any claim, real or assumed, to lifetime or even long-term employment. If conditions or strategic directions change, the employee accepts the possibility that his or her services may no longer be needed.

In return, the company agrees to support, assist, and encourage employees to perfect and maintain their "employability" throughout their tenure with the organization. In doing so, management accepts the premise that an employee's ultimate occupational commitment should be to his or her profession or vocation, not to a single company or even to a single career.

The practical implications of such agreements are likely to be far-reaching. Employers might pledge to inform employees of conditions or decisions that could affect their employment in as timely a manner as possible, for example. This could mean telling an employee that her job might disappear in ten months' time and then supporting her as she searches for a new position, perhaps with a new employer. It could mean providing employees not only with training for job-related skills but also for career-management skills.

Early results indicate that creating this type of trust relationship can have significant implications for organizations and individuals alike: improved productivity and performance on the one hand, plus enhanced career satisfaction and greater career security (a result of improved employability) on the other. But ingraining such behavior in organizational cultures is a tremendous challenge that is sure to take even the most diligent company years to complete.

SURVIVING AND THRIVING AMIDST CONTINUAL CHANGE

WE ARE finally realizing that change just won't go away. To the contrary, we can expect the pace of change to continue to accelerate, while its effect on companies intensifies dramatically. As companies work to seize new competitive opportunities and combat new challenges, the ability to manage change and transition effectively will no longer be considered an arcane, specialized skill, but will shift to become a mainstream responsibility for managers at all levels.

ORDER FORM

Living at the Leading Edge of Change: A Leader's Guide

_____ copies @ $_____ each

Shifting Sands: An Employee Handbook

_____ copies @ $_____ each

1– 99 copies	@$10.95 each
100– 999 copies	@ $9.75 each
1,000– 4,999 copies	@ $7.50 each
5,000– 9,999 copies	@ $6.95 each
10,000 or more copies	@ $5.50 each

To place orders, call toll free 800-345-5627 or drop your order in the mail using this order form. Orders may be faxed to 212-972-2120.

Name_____

Job Title_____

Organization_____

Phone_____

Street Address_____

P.O. Box_____

City, State, ZIP_____

Country_____

Purchase Order Number (if applicable)_____

Applicable sales tax, shipping and handling charges will be added
Prices subject to change.

☐ Check Enclosed   ☐ Please Invoice

☐ Visa   ☐ MasterCard   ☐ American Express

Account Number_____Exp. Date_____

Signature_____